LIFE'S LITTLE
TREASURE BOOK

On Fathers

H. JACKSON BROWN, JR.

RUTLEDGE HILL PRESS®

NASHVILLE, TENNESSEE

Published in Nashville, Tennessee, by Rutledge Hill
Press, Inc., 211 Seventh Avenue North, Nashville,
Tennessee 37219. Distributed in Canada by H. B.
Fenn and Co., Ltd., 34 Nixon Road, Bolton, Ontario
L7E 1W2. Distributed in Australia by The Five Mile
Press Pty., Ltd., 22 Summit Road, Noble Park, Victoria
3174. Distributed in New Zealand by Tandem Press,
2 Rugby Road, Birkenhead, Auckland 10. Distributed
in the United Kingdom by Verulam Publishing, Ltd.,
152a Park Street Lane, Park Street, St. Albans,
Hertfordshire AL2 2AU.

Typography by Compass Communications, Inc.,
Nashville, Tennessee

Photographs by Bob Schatz and are used by
permission.

Book design by Harriette Bateman

ISBN: 1-55853-610-8

Printed in Mexico

1 2 3 4 5 6 7 8 9—02 01 00 99 98

INTRODUCTION

$\mathcal{T}$om Brokaw has compared his experience of being a father to the Energizer bunny—it just keeps going and going and going. It's true; once you are a father, there's no turning back. Your heart strings as well as your purse strings are never again the same.

This little book is offered as a tribute to fathers: those loving and principled men who realize that regardless of how successful they might be at their jobs, their most important and challenging work is done at home.

We're fortunate that fathers offer us experiences and insights quite different from our mothers. While our moms caution us, "Be careful," "Button up," and "Never take a second helping," our dads shout, "Go for it!"

But dads can be nurturing as well as macho. I'm sure many of us remember crawling into our dad's lap to hear for the nine hundredth time his sonorous reading of *Good Night, Moon,* or the feel of his steadying hand on the back fender as we took our first wobbly bicycle ride.

Most of us owe our courage, self-confidence, competitive spirit, and ability to bait our own hooks and to drive a stick shift to our dads. He is teacher, coach, protector, hero, friend, and cheerleader. Whether we call him father, pop, papa, dad, or daddy—he is the Main Man.

$\mathcal{B}$eing a father is like farming—there's always plenty to do.

—HJB

The words a father speaks to his children in the privacy of the home are not overheard at the time, but as in whispering galleries, they will be clearly heard at the end and by posterity.

—Jean Paul Richter

When you want to do something and you're not sure your dad will let you, ask him while he's asleep.

—Age 11

❧

I'll never grow tired of having my dad whisper, "I love you" in my ear.

—Age 39

I was fourteen when my father died. I missed everything about him. He taught us that we shouldn't be people of success, we should be people of values, because that was the only thing that endured.

—Robert F. Kennedy Jr.

*E*ducation is the ability to
listen to almost anything
without losing your temper
or your self-confidence.
—Robert Frost

Favorite quote of Byron Hall's father, Cecil

*W*e judge ourselves by what
we feel capable of doing;
while others judge us by what
we have done.
—Henry Wadsworth Longfellow

Favorite quote of John Duncan's father, Richard

*T*he only means of success is
to render more and better
service than is expected of you,
no matter what your task may
be. This is a habit followed by
all successful people since the
beginning of time. Therefore, I
say the surest way to doom
yourself to mediocrity is to
perform only the work for
which you are paid.

—Og Mandino

Favorite quote of Mary Beth Singer's father, Scott

It is one of the most beautiful compensations of life that no man can sincerely try to help another without helping himself.

—Ralph Waldo Emerson

Favorite quote of Sidney Wail's father, Albert

Sit, walk, or run, but don't wobble.

—Zen Proverb

Favorite quote of Jean Hodgrath's father, David

One of these days in your travels, a guy is going to come up to you and show you a nice, brand-new deck of cards on which the seal is not yet broken. And this guy is going to offer to bet you that he can make the jack of spades jump out of the deck and squirt cider in your ear. But, son, do not bet this man, for as sure as you stand there, you are going to wind up with an earful of cider.

—Advice to Damon Runyon from his father

*M*y father has saved me
from many a foolish act
with these words:
"Go ask your mother."

—Age 16

∽

*T*o really understand how
much my father loves me, I
needed to have a son.

—Age 30

The credit belongs to those who are actually in the arena, who strive valiantly; who know great enthusiasm, the great devotions, and spend themselves in a worthy cause; who at the best, know the triumph of high achievement;

and who, at the worst, if
they fail, fail while daring
greatly, so that their place
shall never be with those
cold and timid souls who
know neither victory
or defeat.

—Theodore Roosevelt

Favorite quote of Rob Shaw's father, Nathan

My dad used to say, "Don't mind a little criticism. It's the sandpaper of life."

—Age 43

Before I got married, I had six theories about bringing up children; now, I have six children and no theories.

—John Wilmot, Earl of Rochester

A wise son makes a glad father.

—Proverbs 10:1

❧

I am grateful to my father for not allowing me to work as a carhop and instead making me work in an office when I was a teenager. Now I am able to count additional experience when applying for a job. It has made the difference in several instances.

—Age 27

$\mathcal{A}$ hug from your daddy
when you are a little girl can
last the rest of your life.

—Age 19

∾

$\mathcal{P}$laying catch with my
father means much more than
most people think.

—Age 15

Never, Never, Never

A Dad's List of Things Not to Do

1. Never speak ill of anyone who has had you as a guest in their home.

2. Never do business with a man who cheats on his wife.

3. Never buy a coffee table you can't put your feet on.

4. Never marry a woman who won't bait her own hook.

5. Never be rude to someone who disappears behind a partition to prepare or deliver your food.

6. Never go up a ladder with just one nail.

7. Never give your wife an anniversary gift that needs to be plugged in.

8. Never hire someone you wouldn't invite home for dinner.

9. Never be photographed with a cocktail glass in your hand.

10. Never say anything uncomplimentary about another person's dog.

11. Never wash a car, mow a yard, or select a Christmas tree after dark.

12. Never forget that it takes only one person or one idea to change your life forever.

There is no such reward for a well-spent life as to see one's children well-started in life, owing to their parents' good health, good principles, fixed character, good breeding, and in general the whole outfit, that enables them to fight the battle of life with success.

—William Graham Sumner

The walks I took with my father around the block on summer nights when I was a child did wonders for me as an adult.

—Age 18

∾

When I want something done around my house, all I have to do is mention to my dad that I'm going to do it myself.

—Age 37

You know you've done
some successful fathering
when you no longer feel
the urge to lead your
children but feel
comfortable walking by
their sides.

*A*s I grow older, I pay less attention to what men say. I just watch what they do.

—Andrew Carnegie

Favorite quote of Suzanne Brewer's father, James

∾

*Y*our enemies will never win as long as you don't hate them back.

—Unknown

Favorite quote of Sam Peterson's father, Christopher

Somebody said that it
   couldn't be done,
But he with a chuckle
   replied
That maybe it couldn't,
   but he would be one
Who wouldn't say so till
   he'd tried.

—Edgar A. Guest

Favorite quote of Howard Samuel's father, Parker

The best advice my father
gave me was his
splendid example.

—Age 18

∞

My hope is that someday my
dad will be as proud of me as
I am of him.

—Age 45

Being a father is the
richest part of my life,
a life that has
exceeded all my
fantasies
of achievement,
fulfillment,
and adventure.

—Tom Brokaw

When I was a boy of fourteen, my father was so ignorant I could hardly stand to have the old man around. But, when I got to be twenty-one, I was astonished at how much he had learned in seven years.

—Mark Twain

$\mathcal{M}$y father used to say that
inflation hasn't ruined
everything. A dime can still be
used as a screwdriver.

—Age 39

❧

$\mathcal{I}$ learned more listening to
my father around the dinner
table than in four years of
college.

—Age 29

*A father is a banker
provided by nature.*

—French Proverb

To Adam

Son, how can I help you see?
May I give you my shoulders
to stand on?
Now you see farther
than me.
Now you see for both of us.
Won't you tell me what
you see?

—HJB

Fathers, do not provoke your children to wrath; but bring them up in the training and admonition of the Lord.

—Ephesians 6:4

❧

The righteous man walks in his integrity; His children are blessed after him.

—Proverbs 20:7

The first time my dad and I had a beer together at my favorite college bar, we learned more about each other that night than in the past twenty-one years.

—Age 21

∾

Dads never put enough mayonnaise on school lunch sandwiches.

—Age 9

Fatherly Advice

- Remain steadfast and loyal to your values.

- Live your life so that someone is always speaking well of you.

- When visiting a foreign country, be on your best behavior. You are an ambassador for your country.

- To find a big opportunity, seek out a big problem.

- Don't forget that right is right even if no one does it, and wrong is wrong even if everyone does it.

- Remember that the biggest challenge you'll ever face is living up to your own potential.

If a man has a talent and cannot use it, he has failed. If he has a talent and uses only half of it, he has partly failed. If he has a talent and learns somehow to use the whole of it, he has gloriously succeeded, and won a satisfaction and a triumph few men ever know.

—Thomas Wolfe

Favorite quote of Susan Schroder's father, Nelson

Work hard.
Aim high.
Play fair.
Help others.

—advice to Adam Brown from his father

Build me a son, O Lord, who will be strong enough to know when he is . . . afraid, one who will be proud and unbending in honest defeat, and humble and gentle in victory.

—Douglas MacArthur, "A Father's Prayer"

❧

No matter how old you get, or how successful you become, you never stop trying to impress your dad.

—Age 48

*The glory
of children
is their father.*

—Proverbs 17:6

Daddy was with me the day I became a daddy and he became a grandpa. I will never forget what my dad said as he held his first grandson in his arms. He looked at me and said, "Bill, you are a rich man."

—Bill Holton,
from *Daddies: An Endangered Species*

Never, Never, Never
A Dad's List of Things Not To Do

1. Never refuse jury duty.

2. Never date anyone who has more than two cats.

3. Never pay for work before it is completed.

4. Never miss a chance to dance with your spouse.

5. Never enter your boss's office without a note pad and pencil.

6. Never let the odds keep you from pursuing what you know in your heart you were meant to do.

7. Never resist a generous impulse.

8. Never order barbeque in a place where all the chairs match.

9. Never marry someone in hopes that he or she will change later.

10. Never buy a Rolex from someone out of breath.

11. Never break off communications with your children no matter what they do.

12. Never drive while holding a cup of hot coffee between your knees.

Life is mostly froth and
bubble;
Two things stand like
stone,
Kindness in another's
trouble,
Courage in our own.

—Adam Gordon

Favorite quote of Vance Tunbull's father, Carl

A spark is a little thing, yet it may kindle the world.

—Martin Farquhar Tupper

Favorite quote of Edward Volkert's father, Don

∾

*P*ractice like a champion.
Play like a champion.
Live like a champion.

—Advice to Adam Brown from his father, Jackson

After you've raised them
Educated them and
gowned them
They just take their little
fingers
And wrap you around them.
Being a father
Is quite a bother
But I like it rather.

—Ogden Nash

The human spirit is stronger than anything that can happen to it.

—C. C. Scott

∾

Duty is the sublimest word in our language. Do your duty in all things. You cannot do more. You should never wish to do less.

—Robert E. Lee

Growing up in Dallas,
I'd often accompany my father to
Clyde's Barber Shop for his twice
monthly hair cut. While he was
getting his trim, I'd get my little
red cowgirl boots shined.
On the way back home we would
stop at Spud Nuts for a bag of
just-from-the-oven doughnuts.
Shiny boots, warm doughnuts,
daddy-daughter talk—it was
just perfect.

—Age 54

Never miss an
opportunity to go
fishing with your father.
—Age 37

As Dad used to say . . .

- When someone says, "trust me," hold on to your wallet.

- When choosing a job, put opportunity ahead of security.

- Don't worry about the mule, just load the wagon.

Set the course of your life by three starts—sincerity, courage, and unselfishness.

—Dr. Monroe Deutsch

Favorite quote of Robert Watt's father, Don

∾

When Plato saw a young boy doing mischief in the streets, he went and corrected the child's father.

Ties

It was
one of
those calls
you don't
expect.

*Dad
how do
you tie
a tie?*

Knowing I
couldn't
do it over
the phone
I said
I'd be
right home.

Standing
eye to eye
with my
little boy
I see myself.

—Ron Turner

from *My Father, My Sons and Me in Between*

Colors fade, temples
crumble, empires fall, but
wise words endure. .

—Edward Thorndike

Favorite quote of Lane Carrey's father, Aaron

$\mathcal{Y}$ou don't have to deserve
your mother's love. You have
to deserve your father's. He's
more particular.

—Robert Frost

It is the calling of the great man, not so much to preach new truths, as to rescue from oblivion those old truths which is our wisdom to remember and our weakness to forget.

—Sydney Smith

Favorite quote of Ellen Scott's father, Robert

When my father and I would go fishing, we seldom caught anything. But it didn't matter to me because the important thing was just having him all to myself.

—Age 41

❧

Saturday morning was pancake breakfast time at our house. Dad would cook and the rest of us would shower him with praise.

—Age 29

My parents gave me wings and sometimes I flew pretty high. But I was confident that should I fall, Daddy would always be there, holding my safety net.

—Age 43

❧

After Dad died, Mom moved his old beat-up recliner to the basement. Sometimes I go down there to sit in it. It still smells of his pipe and old favorite sweater.

—Age 55

It is no use walking
anywhere to preach unless
our walking is our preaching.

—Saint Francis of Assisi

Favorite quote of Barbara Fairfax's father, Frank

❧

I destroy my enemy by
making him my friend.

—Abraham Lincoln

Favorite quote of Will Long's father, Newman

The most important domestic challenge facing the U.S. at the close of the twentieth century is the re-creation of fatherhood as a vital social role for men. At stake is nothing less than the success of the American experiment.

—David Blakenhorn

*W*hen it [fatherhood] is experienced, it makes you one with all men in a way that fills you with warmth and harmony.

—Kurt Newbum

∾

*B*eing a father is the most frustrating, challenging, exasperating job I've ever loved.

—B. C. Daily

I've learned that . . .

. . . my father lets me do things my mother would never think about. —Age 13

. . . my daddy says a lot of words that I can't. —Age 8

. . . I may never be wealthy, but because of the love and guidance my father gave me, I'll be forever rich. —Age 29

Do not pray for easy lives.
Pray to be stronger men!
Do not pray for tasks equal to
your powers.
Pray for powers equal to
your tasks.

—Phillip Brooks

Favorite quote of Leigh Kiser's father, Robert

∾

My dad is stronger than
Superman and funnier than
Big Bird.

—Age 7

I can compare my childhood to listening to a radio. My mother selected the station but my father set the volume.

—HJB

❧

Nothing I've ever done has given me more joy and rewards than being a father to my five.

—Bill Cosby

It is the greatest of all
mistakes to do nothing
because you can only do a
little. Do what you can.

—Sydney Smith

Favorite quote of Graham Beaman's father,
Kenneth

❧

Death is not the greatest loss
in life. The greatest loss
is what dies within us while
we live.

—Norman Cousins

Favorite quote of John Raine's father, Barry

Fatherly Advice

- Sing out in church; God isn't a music critic.

- Remember that the quickest way to get a raise is to raise your commitment to the company.

- Find a reputable car shop before you need one.

- Unplug all appliances before leaving on a trip.

- Take good care of the kid inside you.

- Remember, it doesn't help to have a road map if your car won't start.

- When you meet people you admire, ask them the books they are currently reading.

- Don't put the candy dish next to the phone.

- Keep the chase in your marriage.

$\mathcal{B}$e an example of what you want to see more of in the world.

—Advice to Virginia Talmadge from her dad

❧

$\mathcal{T}$he most important thing a father can do for his children is to love their mother.

—Theodore Martin Hesburgh

What you can do,

or dream you can,

begin it.

Boldness has genius,

power, and magic

in it.

—Johann Wolfgang von Goethe

Favorite quote of Mary Sherwood's father, Addison

My wife and I have five children. To have their respect is the ultimate hall of fame. They see it all. They see how you treat each other. Getting and keeping their respect is what really matters. The question we must continually ask ourselves is, "How do we get to where we want to go and still remain a hero to those we love?"

—Roger Staubach

If you can keep your head
when all about you
Are losing theirs and blaming
it on you;
If you can trust yourself when
all men doubt you,
But make allowance for their
doubting too;

If you can fill the unforgiving
minute
With sixty seconds' worth of
distance run—
Yours is the Earth and
everything that's in it,
And—which is more—you'll
be a Man, my son!

—Rudyard Kipling

Favorite quote of Larry Hewlett's father, Michael

The heights by great men
    reached and kept
Were not attained by sudden
    flight,
But they, while their
    companions slept,
Were toiling upward in the
    night.

—Henry Wadsworth Longfellow

Favorite quote of Dan Ingersoll's father, Dale

$\mathcal{M}$y father and I once rearranged the living room furniture while my mom was away visiting my aunt. When she returned, she almost had a cow.

—Age 27

❧

$\mathcal{D}$ad had a fool-proof way of cooking steaks: After one beer, turn them over; after two beers, take them off the grill—they're ready.

—Age 61

Dad's 21 Suggestions for Success

1. Marry the right person. This one decision will determine 90 percent of your happiness or misery.

2. Work at something you enjoy and thats worthy of your time and talent.

3. Give people more than they expect and do it cheerfully.

4. Become the most positive and enthusiastic person you know.

5. Be forgiving of yourself and others.

6. Be generous.

7. Have a grateful heart.

8. Persistence, persistence, persistence.

9. Discipline yourself to save money on even the most modest salary.

10. Understand that happiness is not based on possessions, power, or prestige, but on relationships with people you love and respect.

11. Be loyal

12. Be honest.

13. Be a self-starter.

14. Treat everyone you meet as you want to be treated.

15. Commit yourself to constant improvement.

16. Commit yourself to quality.

17. Stop blaming others. Take responsibility for every area of your life.

18. Be bold and courageous. When you look back on your life, you'll regret the things you didn't do more than the ones you did.

19. Be decisive even if it means you'll sometimes be wrong.

20. Take good care of those you love.

21. Don't do anything that wouldn't make your Mom proud.

—HJB

The only thing necessary for the triumph of evil is for good men to do nothing.

—Edmund Burke

Favorite quote of Pamela Copeland's father, Howard

No man who is occupied in doing a very difficult thing, and in doing it well, ever loses his self respect.

—George Bernard Shaw

Favorite quote of Steven Conway's father, Gerald

$\mathscr{T}$wo roads diverged in the wood, and I—
I took the one less traveled by,
And that has made all the difference.

—Robert Frost

Favorite quote of Jennifer Higgins's father, Perry

∾

$\mathscr{N}$othing happens unless first a dream.

—Carl Sandburg

Favorite quote of Benjamin Divita's father, Paul

A Father's Toast to His Son

May your adversities
 make you strong.

May your victories
 make you wise.

May your actions
 make you proud.

—HJB

$\mathscr{M}$ake no little plans; they have no magic to stir men's blood.

—Daniel Hudson Burnham

Favorite quote of Rosemary Newhouse's father, Peter

∾

$\mathscr{Y}$ou'll never get anywhere if you don't take a chance.

—Advice to Tyler Calloway from his father, Steven

Life doesn't come with an instruction book. That's why we have fathers.